A Manifesto for Growing Leaders on Your Campus

Published in Atlanta, Georgia, by Poet Gardener Publishing in association with Growing Leaders, Inc.

www.GrowingLeaders.com

ISBN: 978-0-9832031-0-0

Printed in the United States of America

Library of Congress Cataloguing-in-Publication Data

Contents

An Introduction

I have wanted to write this manifesto for years. In fact, ever since I first began having conversations with deans, headmasters, and other school administrators about cultivating leaders among their student body, I have yearned to put in print the thoughts I shared with them.

Today, it isn't enough for schools to create a leadership-training event or program. It's insufficient to host a conference for leaders in the fall, and hope that students will remain equipped and motivated to carry out their leadership positions during that school year. In reality, I am not sure if that ever worked. Leadership development must be organic, flowing from the very culture of the campus. A leadership bias must be in the DNA of the administration; it must be central to the organizational values, and implemented in a plan that flows out of the lives of those nearest to the students.

I first began to implement the ideas in this Manifesto more than 25 years ago, when I was a young leader myself, overseeing a college and career department at Skyline Church in San Diego. Within seven years, our weekly class grew from an average size of 60 to over 600. I'm convinced it wasn't because I was such a good teacher. It was because we developed great student leaders. One in every ten students served in a leadership role. Most of the remaining population thought like a leader and were leaders in their own right. We developed a plan to grow leaders.

This manifesto is designed to provide that philosophy and plan. It is one flowing conversation where I will lay out foundations for healthy leader development among the emerging generation. In addition, I will furnish ideas for how to sponsor training that results in real life-change—organic rather than programmatic—and I will lay out steps you can take to cultivate a leadership culture on your campus or in your organization.

I hope you have as much fun processing these concepts as I did writing them.

Tim Elmore
Atlanta, GA
December 2010

Why Is the Task of Growing Leaders so Important?

It's a good question to begin with.

Why is this issue so paramount? Why all the fuss about leadership? To be honest, I've spoken to some school teachers and youth workers who say it's just a fad. Some also say too much emphasis is placed on leadership; and it's exclusive—it leaves some kids out of the picture. When I talk further with these people, we discover our definitions for leadership are different. In this manifesto, you will see that my definition for leadership is completely inclusive. It simply challenges students to become the best version of themselves possible, and to leverage positive influence on others. More about that later.

In six brief statements, I have outlined why the task of growing leaders is so vital to the future. These are actually case statements as to why our organization exists. Our purpose is to turn ordinary students into growing leaders who will transform society. The task of growing leaders is vital. Here's why I believe this responsibility should be front and center:

1. Because we are at a critical point in history... if we don't act now, when will we?

Our world faces a moral crisis. We are in a cultural war against principles—leaving many with no moral compass to evaluate their direction. The AIDS pandemic in Africa, the sex trade among children in Asia, terrorism in the Middle East, drug traffic in Latin America, poverty in half the world's nations and the moral vacuum in America and Europe are cries for healthy, effective leaders to provide direction. Even in the U.S., 62 percent of kids are being raised without their biological father. Models and values are often missing. It isn't enough to add followers. We must multiply quality leaders.

2. Because kids are our future... what will happen if we fail to prepare them?

Today, almost one half the world's population is 21 years old or younger. This means that three to four billion young people are in need of being developed. Ready or not, they will lead our world into the future. Sadly, we've done more protecting than preparing. Members of the Millennial generation (born between 1984-2002), are hungry to change the world. While they can be self-absorbed and impatient, they are optimistic, social, and savvy with technology. It is our responsibility to prepare them to lead the way. It is easier to shape a child than to rebuild an adult.

3. Because students need a process—not just an event... how can mere events mentor them?

We believe leaders are not raised up in crowds, but through life-on-life mentoring relationships. Older generations must invest in younger ones. Our goal is to see students transformed from the inside out so they can turn their world upside down. They don't want a sage on the stage but a guide on the side. *Harvard Business Review* surveyed top business leaders and discovered every CEO had but one item in common. Each had a mentor. Half of the Nobel Peace Prize winners were mentored by former peace prize laureates. Mentoring is the key. It's a process, not an event.

4. Because we're heading toward a leadership vacuum... who will replace the retiring generation?

In the next fifteen years, 45 percent of the workforce in the U.S. will be disappearing. The Baby Boomers, which make up the majority of this group, are retiring and vacating their leadership roles in business, in government, in education, in churches, and as missionaries. These vacancies must be filled by young, trained leaders. Why? Leaders provide solutions. That's what our world needs most—a new batch of problem-solving leaders. According to research done at the Higher Education Research Institute, leadership qualities can no longer be the property of the elite few. In today's world, every student will need to learn leadership skills.

5. Because an ounce of prevention is worth a pound of cure... can we afford to wait for a crisis?

There are many great causes with which to join hands. If we only feed, clothe and house the needy, however, we'll merely put a band-aid on the problems we face. We must focus on the future. If we can equip young people with new habits and attitudes, we will prevent problems for years to come. We'll be playing offense, not defense. It is better to build a fence at the top of the cliff, than a hospital at the bottom. We want to address the crises before they begin, by preparing young people to be leaders.

6. Because culture-shaping movements often begin with the young... isn't it time for one?

Our world doesn't need another program—we need a movement. A cursory study of history reveals that many of the movements that changed the world began with young people. From Jesus and His disciples, to Joan of Arc, to William Wilberforce, to John Wesley, to Martin Luther King, Jr.—nations have been impacted by young adults. We believe it is time for another movement that will transform society. We also believe if we have any chance of seeing it happen today, we must reach out to the next generation.

What We See in the Future

This is what we must be about, as educators, employers, coaches, and youth workers. When I look into the future, I see millions of young people who finally caught a vision for what their life could count for. They've moved from complacent gamers or Facebook junkies to engaged change-agents. They embrace adulthood and decide they can, indeed, transform society. They see an inward picture that ignites an inward passion. They've discovered their gift, and decided to serve it up to the world. In a term, they become *life-giving leaders:*

Their ambition is service, not money.
Their motive is compassion, not competition.
They think out of the box and are not limited by protocol.
They hunger for influence, not mere existence.
They plan to solve a problem, not just sell a product.
They are about a work, not just a job.

I envision graduating students who've caught a vision for the importance of thinking and acting like a life-giving leader. Because of this vision, I see the following:

• A handful of young adults from different disciplines—business, biology, chemistry, social work, medicine, and education—discover a cure for cancer, diabetes, and the AIDS virus.

• A large cadre of grads utilizing their education to solve the hunger problem among starving people groups. They identify a way to provide food for everyone.

• A young person finds a way to provide teaching and training for African nations that transforms corrupt cultures and nurtures a healthy leadership culture.

• A group of students work so hard to get clean water in Rwanda, Ghana, Botswana, and other nations that they develop a system to create wells across the continent.

• An online community of twenty-somethings is so committed to stopping the sex trade that it dries up globally; offenders are either arrested or leave the trade.

• A huge population of brilliant graduates transforms the educational system in the U.S. They commit to teach in underfunded school districts, turning at-risk kids into college graduates.

• A swelling demographic of youth from all backgrounds decide to plant new churches and mission outreaches that meet the needs of underprivileged people.

• A globally connected community of young people join an online conversation, and agree that terrorism is antiquated and must be stopped. Pressure builds and they succeed.

Join us as we equip these future heroes.

For Discussion

1. What are your dreams and vision for the youth on your campus, organization, or ministry?
2. Would you agree that the task of growing leaders is vital for our future?

Is Everyone a Leader?

There I stood in front of a crowd of one thousand students and faculty members at a university in the Midwest. One instructor stood up with a question I get almost everywhere I go. Usually it is asked by a person who already has an answer—they just want to hear what I'm going to say to this seemingly obvious question . . .

"Is everyone a leader?"

The answer, of course, is yes and no. (How's that for a politically correct response?) It all depends on how you define the word "leader." If you define it in the traditional fashion—that a leader is someone with a position, in charge of a group of people in an organization—then, the answer is no, in my opinion. Not everyone and certainly not every student is gifted to become the president, the chairman, the CEO, or the top leader of a large team of people. Most will never occupy a top spot in a flow chart. Perhaps only ten percent of the population will. For the sake of discussion, we'll call these people "Leaders" with a capital "L."

If leadership means possessing a gift to organize groups of people to accomplish a task, then it's exclusive and obviously not for everyone. In fact, we will frustrate students by telling them they are "Leaders"—only to disappoint them with a lofty ideal they'll never attain. We create a false expectation. Most of the arguments surrounding this question boil down to contrasting definitions.

If we define leadership, however, in a different manner, it opens up an entirely new perspective for students. What if leadership was more about people pursuing a "calling" in their life; a calling with which they will influence others in its fulfillment? What if it had more to do with finding an area of strength—and in using that strength, they'll naturally influence others in a positive way? The ancient Hebrews had a way of looking at this from a spiritual perspective. Consider this passage from the very first book in their Pentateuch: *"And God said, 'Let us make man in our image and in our likeness, and let him rule the earth..."*

They taught that their Maker created mankind in His image. What does it mean to be made in the image of God? Part of the meaning is furnished in the very next phrase: "*...and let him rule.*" Rabbis taught that part of what it means to be made in the image of God is that humans have the capacity to lead and to rule the earth.

It seems to me, every one of us possesses some strength or gift that enables us to master something and to exercise dominion in a healthy way. Certainly, mankind has perverted this idea of dominion. History is full of leaders who tried to dominate others by force, such as Nero, Stalin, Hitler, and Saddam Hussein. But we cannot let counterfeits of good leadership convince us that leadership should be avoided. In fact, if there is a counterfeit, it generally means something genuine exists that is very valuable. Leadership was intended to be about serving others in the area of our giftedness. When we do, we naturally ripple with influence. We don't even have to try to "lead" others. As we mature, we are to naturally uncover our area of dominion and influence a sum of people. We may not even have a position at the top of a flow chart, but we lead.

Because this is a larger segment of the population, it might be helpful to call these people "leaders" with a lower case "l." They are "leaders," not "Leaders." They are everywhere, and we must prepare them to influence their world. This is why I choose to define leadership in this way:

Leadership is leveraging my influence for a worthwhile cause.

Let me say it another way. These two kinds of leaders ("Leaders" and "leaders") can be defined as HABITUAL leaders and SITUATIONAL leaders. "Habitual leaders" are the natural ones, who tend to be good at leading whatever group they are in. They feel natural taking charge and running point on just about any project. They lead out of habit. "Situational leaders" are those people who make up the majority of the population. Most of them don't even feel like leaders—until they find the right situation that fits their passions and their strengths. Once in the area of their strength, they come alive and become the right one to lead in that particular situation. This is why a central goal for mentors ought to be to help emerging leaders find their "situation." This situation is likely where a person will fulfill their purpose and leverage their best influence.

Gotta Have It

In 2000, the Higher Education Research Institute published a report on the status of leadership on university campuses in North America. The report included both state and private schools. It was sponsored by the Kellogg Foundation and was compiled by Dr. Helen and Alexander Astin, founders of H.E.R.I. at UCLA. Their conclusions were intriguing. Let me summarize a few of them here:

- Every student has leadership potential.
- Leadership cannot be separated from values.
- Leadership skills must be taught.
- In today's world, every student will need leadership skills.

Interestingly, it seems that I'm not the only one who's concluded that leadership should not be limited to the people who hold top positions in an organization. More and more agree that leadership is a 360-degree proposition. Most people who influence where teams, corporations, or non-profits are going—in fact, where nations are going—are not the Chief Executives of those organizations. We lead up, we lead around, and we lead down in organizations. Dee Hock, former CEO of Visa International was the first person I heard propose this notion, and I believe he's right on.

Influence happens everywhere—and often from the middle of the pack. This is why I teach that every student who is willing has the potential to lead and influence others. They may never be "Leaders" but they are already "leaders."

Sociologists believe the most introverted of people will influence 10,000 others in an average lifetime.

In others words, every one of us, even the shy ones, are influencing the people around us. My question is, what breadth of influence could people have who become intentional about it?

Naturally, some folks are going to turn out to be better leaders than others. Some will actually become excellent at organizing large teams of people, or speaking to large groups of people and casting vision to them. But leadership isn't limited to these skills. If it's only for the skilled people, then we'll never accomplish the good that needs to happen in our lifetime. It would be like saying that no one has to donate if they don't have a lot of money, or no one has to serve others if they have no great talent. That's ludicrous. We all have the responsibility to do what we can—based upon our level of gifts and strengths.

So, let's embrace it. Let's learn to lead and influence in a manner appropriate with our giftedness, and not excuse ourselves because we'll never be Mother Teresa, Martin Luther King, Jr., Steve Jobs, or Bill Gates. Leadership is a calling on every one of us, to some degree. It's about becoming the person we were designed to be. It is less about position and more about disposition. It is not so much about superiority, but it's about service in the area of our strengths. It has less to do with a set of behaviors and more to do with a perspective with which we view life.

When we define leadership this way, it puts the cookies on the bottom shelf. Every one of us can do it.

For Discussion

1. How do you define leadership? Do you believe every student has some influence to leverage?
2. How do you foster an environment that encourages students to think and act like leaders?
3. Do you believe your school or organization embraces the idea that leadership potential lies inside of each student?
4. Are you ready to move forward with a plan to equip and inspire the leadership qualities in students?

How to Spot a Leader Early

If we're serious about growing leaders on the campus, we must get serious about defining the outcomes we're pursuing, and about determining what we're looking for in students. I believe there are some raw materials inside students that provide early clues about leadership predisposition. We accelerate our progress if we can spot them early. Let me illustrate.

In 1921, Franklin Delano Roosevelt was diagnosed with polio. It was a deadly disease until 1957. The diagnosis changed any expectations of a normal life for an adult. Polio crippled nearly everyone who contracted it. Most recognized they were destined for life in a wheelchair.

At the same time, a friend of Roosevelt's contracted polio as well. The two men drew closer to each other having a shared disability and common struggle. While both young men ended up in a wheelchair, their lives turned out radically different. FDR's friend took the "road most traveled." He slowly became passive about his condition. Eventually, he grew bitter and even angry at his handicap. It is easy to understand. He was never able to do the sort of things that young men do with women, with sports, and with their vocation. Roosevelt's friend shrunk from ever expecting anything worthwhile of himself, and eventually died an unknown and quite melancholy death.

In contrast, Roosevelt somehow decided to make the most of his situation. You might say he took the "road less traveled." He had this gnawing belief in his gut that he was supposed to amount to something and positively influence others. He ended up seeing his disablement as a way to identify with the outcasts in society. He allowed it to give him courage. After entering a career in civil service, he later went into politics. The disease actually helped him reach his goals. Franklin D. Roosevelt served as our U.S. president during the Great Depression and World War II. He became the only president elected to four terms of office.

I've often asked myself how two individuals with similar circumstances could reach such contrasting outcomes. Roosevelt's friend had every reason to be bitter and end up merely surviving such a hellish childhood. He was a victim of his circumstances. Roosevelt, however, was different. He refused to be merely a victim. FDR grew through his circumstances and became an effective leader during a most difficult period in our country's history.

Roosevelt's is not an isolated story. Other incredible leaders in history fought horrific diseases during their early years. Sir Isaac Newton, Michelangelo, and Leonardo Da Vinci all had epilepsy. Abraham Lincoln struggled with chronic depression. Thomas Edison and Ludwig van Beethoven were both deaf. Harriet Tubman was vision impaired, and Galileo went completely blind. For some reason, the struggle did not diminish them. Their leadership rose above it all.

Three Intrinsic Signals

As I study young people and attempt to instill leadership qualities in them, I have drawn a conclusion. While I believe every child and young adult has influence and can learn to be a leader, I believe there are at least three intrinsic leadership signals that some kids send to their parents and teachers as early as the third and fourth grade. They're the same signals that FDR, Newton, and Lincoln must have sent as kids. They can be seen as children interact with both peers and adults.

1. Perception

The first leadership signal youth demonstrate surrounds the way they think. They perceive the world a bit differently than the majority of their peers. They are able to see a bigger picture. While they remain most concerned with their own needs, their perspective extends beyond those needs. They see how situations impact others around them. They are able to fly 30,000 feet above the ground, and get a bird's eye view of those situations and respond accordingly.

This can show up in a number of ways. A ten-year-old may arrive at a restaurant with her parents, knowing they'll be meeting up with friends or extended family for a meal. Without instruction, she enters the restaurant determining how big the table must be, and how many chairs they'll need to request of the hostess. That's an early signal of leadership. It all begins with perception.

2. Responsibility

This is a second signal kids send to adults that leadership qualities exist innately within them. They feel responsible for outcomes. Even as young children, they assume they must help solve problems, correct false statements, or even serve someone who cannot do something for themselves. Often, these students pay attention to details, and seem to care about elements their peers might find trivial or not worth their attention. At other times, their sense of responsibility isn't displayed in details as much as an effort to make sure the final, desired goal is reached.

The Gallup Organization created an instrument years ago called Strengths Finder. One of the 34 internal strengths that humans possess is: responsibility. Those who demonstrate responsibility are often an establishment's best workers. At Growing Leaders, we seldom hire staff or interns if they don't display responsibility as one of their top five strengths. It is the natural bent to cover bases and make things right even without being told to do so.

3. Initiative

A third leadership signal young people demonstrate is initiative. This is the internal drive to act. When they perceive something could be done to improve conditions, they believe it should be done and they step out first to do it. They don't necessarily wait for peers to approve. At times, they don't even wait to see if their behavior is the norm or is safe. They go first.

This can lead students to do some very stupid things—things they might get punished for—because they can't stand the current conditions. But we must remember: it is an early sign of leadership. The young person's perception is clear and their dissatisfaction is compelling. I've known kids to get involved with recycling bottles, raising money for a friend who has cancer, or even collecting clothes and food for Haiti because they have a strong sense of initiative.

My Takeaway

I believe there are two obvious action steps I can take as an adult who wishes to build leadership skills in students. First, I can look for these three intrinsic qualities in students, and position them in authentic leadership roles. Second, I can nurture these qualities in my own kids and in the students around me. These qualities (perception, responsibility, and initiative) are life skills we must not fail to develop in our future leaders.

The qualities are not difficult to see. Students who possess them will demonstrate problem-solving skills as they encounter challenges. They will be a source of solutions. In short, they will:

- See it. (Perception)
- Own it. (Responsibility)
- Do it. (Initiative)

I've given my life to foster these qualities in the next generation of young people. Will you join me?

For Discussion

1. Have you seen these three qualities in any non-positioned student?
2. Do you believe there are other essential predictors of leadership potential?
3. How could you incorporate these qualities in your selection process?

Characteristics of a Growing Leader

I have worked with students since 1979—and over that period of time, I have set new goals and focused my efforts accordingly. At first, I just wanted kids to like me. I wanted the students I worked with to enjoy my leadership, engage with my teaching and to have a good time. Within a few years, I determined I had to pursue a bigger goal. I began to push them to grow and mature. This was a good beginning for me to expand my vision. Over time, however, I realized that while this is a good goal, it still wasn't enough. I began to mobilize students to serve. Surely, this is what student development was all about.

While I continue to mobilize students to serve the world they live in—I have concluded there is still something more. Service must have an outcome. We must grow servant-leaders. The University of Maryland calls this the "social change model." Service must lead to some kind of positive change. I suppose one could argue that all service does, indeed, positively transform the world in some way. But I believe we must think and act strategically. How can our service be rendered to achieve the greatest amount of good?

Strategic service can be defined as a key act, at a key time, addressing a key need.

For instance, I could clean up a local pond which accomplishes a little good. Or, I could provide a service that multiplies itself and does a greater good, which is the more strategic option. I must think about the influence of my service; the results it will accomplish. That's just plain wisdom. It doesn't mean that certain service roles are beneath me. It simply means I will render strategic service whenever possible. I will do the greatest amount of good I can with the gifts and time I have. I don't merely render "random acts of kindness" but strategic acts of kindness. Busyness is not my goal. Growing leaders should work to transform the world in which they live.

What Are We Trying to Build?

This is what I am about. This is why some of us launched our organization in 2003. We are trying to build "growing leaders." They will stand in contrast to their peers around the world. They will be counter-cultural. They are marked by these characteristics:

Ordinary Students	Growing Leaders
1. Self-absorbed	1. Sacrificial
2. Imitate others	2. Authentic
3. Apathetic	3. Committed
4. Consuming	4. Generous
5. Presumptuous	5. Grateful
6. Controlling	6. Empowering
7. Status quo	7. Hungry mind
8. What can I get?	8. What can I give?
9. It's about the money	9. It's about a mission
10. Blend in	10. Stand out

These words describe the mission at "Growing Leaders," our non-profit organization. Growing leaders are who we target. Growing leaders is what we do. Growing leaders are the end result of all our efforts.

We want to unleash an entire generation of young people who find their gifts and give them away to a needy world—in the most strategic way possible.

They are students who are aware of their influence and leverage it wisely.

Needless to say, "growing leaders" are different. They stand out because of their different approach to life and leadership. Most people see themselves changing from the outside in. It's all about appearance and behavior modification to get what you want. Growing Leaders believes real change happens from the inside out. It's about changing the heart—our habits and attitudes—in order to experience real transformation. We can only pass on what we have ourselves. Only the transformed can transform others.

Join the revolution.

For Discussion

1. How do schools today become consumed with survival rather than developing young leaders?
2. What do you do to equip young people to think and act like servant-leaders?
3. If you were to divide the students on your campus into two groups, how many do you believe exhibit the "growing leaders" characteristics? How many fit more with the characteristics in the "ordinary students" column?

How Do Ordinary Students Become Growing Leaders?

In 2009, a movie hit the box offices around the U.S. It was called, "Defiance." The movie told the history of hundreds of Jewish refugees who avoided capture by the Nazi's during World War II, in Belarus. It's a poignant true story of leadership during a time of chaos. Daniel Craig played the role of Tuvia Bielski, and Live Schreiber played the role of his brother, Zus. These men struggle with how to best navigate the future of this growing band of resistants. There were no titles or badges naming who should be in charge—and the brothers' convictions were sharply different. The whole story got me thinking—how do leaders emerge? How do we spot them? On what path do they step forward for all to see? How do ordinary people become leaders that others will follow?

Both you and your students are on a leadership journey. As you become intentional about this journey on your campus, let me suggest four paths that individuals take on their way to becoming a leader. Maybe you can spot these in your organization or school.

1. SOME ARE GIFTED TO LEAD. *(They are enabled by their ability.)*

These are the easiest kind of emerging leaders to identify. They are people who simply possess the ability to lead. Either because of their personality or because they have the talent to organize or plan a strategy. These people step up and find it natural to lead, regardless of the circumstance. Whatever team they are on, whatever group they are in—they seem to be the person that others look to for answers. They usually have a strong personality. They often are gifted at articulating key goals. They are almost always clear on what must happen to reach those goals.

I have worked alongside Dr. John C. Maxwell since 1983. John is this kind of leader. If you assembled a group of people in a room—and you placed Dr. Maxwell in that room with them, he would inevitably take charge. I don't mean this in a derogatory way. He is just gifted to lead. He does it naturally. He has the ability to quickly see what needs to happen to reach a target or make things run more efficiently. He also has the strength to attract people to his plan. He is magnetic. I have seen John organize travelers at an airport, when the flight was delayed and come up with a plan to get to their destination. I have watched him turn a chaotic situation at a restaurant into one of laughter and cooperation; he turns groups into teams. He steps up to lead because of his gift.

2. SOME ARE SITUATED TO LEAD. *(They are enabled by an opportunity.)*

The gifted leader makes up, perhaps 10-15 percent of the population. If leading is reserved for gifted individuals—we'll without a doubt experience more problems than solutions. There just aren't enough gifted leaders to go around. Fortunately, this isn't the case. Earlier, I said I believe there are two kinds of leaders—and everyone fits into one of these two categories: habitual leaders and situational leaders. Habitual leaders are the ones we just discussed above. They lead out of habit. Situational leaders are the ones who don't believe they're a leader—but, put them in the right situation and they lead. Find a situation that matches who they are—their strengths, their passion and abilities—and in that situation, they will know what to do. And they will influence others.

My daughter, Bethany, is a situational leader. She would be the first to admit she isn't the world's greatest leader. Her personality is very phlegmatic. She's laid-back, casual, and simply enjoys relationships. However, as a Resident Advisor at her university—she finds herself in a situation that matches her identity. She is natural at leading her floor of women. She has intuition about people, she is comfortable in meetings, she's confident, she's socially aware, and she experiences her deepest influence in that situation. It's her sweet spot.

3. Some are positioned to lead. *(They are enabled by some authority.)*

There is a third path to leadership. An organization has a vacant role that must be filled and they place a person in that role to see what happens. Sometimes, they're merely looking for a warm body to meet a need, or a person to temporarily "plug a hole" in the boat. Often when the potential leader steps into the position—it brings the best out in them. A sense of initiative and responsibility surface, and they rise to the occasion. Perhaps those virtues would have never been so visible had it not been for the new "title" and position. Although I do believe there are many people with leadership positions who are not fit to lead—and that a position does not automatically make a leader—still there are some that only lead well once they are given the authority to do so.

For years, I taught college students in San Diego. Richard was a student who entered our department as a quiet, unassuming, and shy young man. The last word you would use to describe him was the word: leader. However, as time went on, I noticed his high level of integrity and his follow through on every assignment. I felt he would make a great study group leader—and so I asked him to become one. He was reluctant. He didn't see himself as a leader at all. In fact, he called himself a "follower." I replied that following well was the first step on the leadership journey. Richard finally gave in and led a group. He was outstanding. The next year, he was leading three groups; by his final year in school, he was leading all the study group leaders. Even he was surprised. It was in him all the time—he just needed to be positioned correctly.

4. Some are summoned to lead. *(They are enabled by a crisis.)*

This fourth pathway is most intriguing. I believe many potential leaders step into their primary means of influence because they are "summoned" by the circumstances around them. In other words, many people view themselves as quite "ordinary." It is only when a crisis occurs or a tragedy looms on the horizon, that we see what's really inside those ordinary people. Do you remember those who responded to the terrorist attacks on 9/11 or Hurricane Katrina? Those folks weren't seeking a title, nor were they seeking greatness or notoriety. When a problem arises, however, these people see clearly what must happen, and they step up to the plate. They don't even think of themselves as a leader when they move into action. They just know someone has to do something, and instead of looking around for someone else to do it . . . they look inside and lead the way.

In his early days, Harry Truman was summoned to lead. As a kid, he was a geek. He worked on a farm, although he wasn't big or well built. Furthermore, he wore thick eye-glasses that resembled the bottom of a Coke bottle. While in college—his father became ill, so he returned home and never completed his studies. It was while this nerdy young man served in the military during World War I that he saw who he was. His troop was marching through Europe when German artillery began dropping all around them. Nearly every soldier ran in retreat. Harry Truman's horse fell over almost killing him. But he slipped out from underneath, stood up, and yelled for the men to get back in formation. They had a mission to fulfill. Those men were stunned to hear this quiet, unintimidating "four-eyed" man calling them to finish what they'd started. They returned and followed Truman's instructions. Later in his diary, he wrote: "I learned two things about myself that night. One, I had a little courage. And two, I liked to lead others." As president, he handled some of the toughest decisions ever made by a leader.

Every person's life is an ongoing story. And everyone's life is a path to somewhere. Most of us accumulate influence along the way. May you be able to see your path and the paths of students around you clearly—and help them become the leaders they were meant to become.

For Discussion

1. When you consider your current student leaders, which path have they taken to become a leader?
2. Have you created places for students to "discover" leadership potential inside?
3. What paths must you still develop for students to find where they fit?

Guiding Principles to Grow Leaders

Good parents embrace a philosophy for raising their children. Good coaches possess a philosophy for leading their athletic teams. Good teachers, along the way, figure out the pedagogy that works best for them in the classroom. Sadly, many institutions of higher education have etched the words, "Building Tomorrow's Leaders" on the marble walls of their administration building, but have no plan to do it. I know. I have asked hundreds of deans, directors, principals, and college presidents. It's a mission they hope to accomplish by merely asking their students to attend class and study for the exams.

If we're going to build leaders, we've got to have a plan. Before we examine some ideas for a healthy, relevant philosophy of leader development, however, let's examine what many schools, organizations, businesses, and churches are presently doing that doesn't work. Our current mode of operation is failing.

Left-Brain Schools in a Right-Brain World

I remember an activity from my early childhood. When we were in elementary school, my sisters and I used to play "school." We'd get the chalkboard out, the chairs, and the map—and one of us would be the teacher. Sometimes we'd get the G.I. Joe's or stuffed animals involved to enlarge the class size a bit. When we didn't know what we were doing, we never lost our passion. We just got creative and made something up. It was a blast.

Over time, I noticed my whole perspective changed. School became somewhat of a drudgery. I stopped "playing" school. More than that, however, I stopped looking forward to it and began looking for ways to get out of it. Sadly, I was like most kids. School and learning were fun when we were young, but eventually they came to mean irrelevance and boredom. For many, school is even repulsive.

I know what some of you are thinking. Education isn't meant to be fun. That's not its purpose. Education is not entertainment. Agreed. The purpose of school is not pleasure and amusement. However, based on our research, education that sticks in the minds of students is usually connected to three elements:

- A healthy, trusting relationship with the teacher.
- An interactive learning community.
- Creativity and innovation that stimulate the "right-brain."

Maya Angelou wrote, "We are all creative, but by the time we are three or four years old, someone has knocked the creativity out of us. Some people shut up the kids who start to tell stories. Kids dance in their cribs, but someone will insist they sit still. By the time the creative people are ten or twelve, they want to be like everyone else."

In Your Right Brain

Daniel Pink has written some helpful insights about how our brains function in his book, *A Whole New Mind*. In it, he describes the difference between left-brain thinking and right-brain thinking. He argues that the old world is a left-brain world. The new one is a right-brain world. Let me summarize part of the problem with education in one phrase: we are preparing students in "left-brain" schools to enter a "right-brain" world. The school does not resemble the world they will enter after graduation, if they graduate at all.

The left brain is about KNOWLEDGE. *The right brain is about* IMAGINATION.

The left-brain is calculated and definitive. The right-brain is innovative and dynamic. One is about cognition. The other is about creativity. Certainly both are necessary. But more and more, our world is driven by right-brain thought. Sadly, consider what's happening today in schools. With a poor economy, budget cuts are being made all over the country. The first courses dropped by public schools are right- brain courses: art, music, and drama.

Albert Einstein once said, "Imagination is more important than knowledge." What he meant was knowledge is finite. Imagination can take a person into the infinite. Knowledge includes only what's already developed. Imagination is about our dreams, which have no limits. Unfortunately, our educational institutions revolve around self-contained silos of existing information. They're about lecture, drill, and test. Testing involves students regurgitating facts they've heard from instructors that semester. Nothing more. Nothing less.

I had the privilege of meeting with the Georgia Teachers of the Year. After our training time, I realized one of the chief reasons these faculty members were chosen as "the best" was that they included a balance of right-brain and left-brain methods. Several of them confirmed my suspicions:

- Schools often teach and test for questions that aren't relevant.
- Schools only drill for memory rather than critical thinking.
- School departments function independently, not providing the big picture.
- Schools prepare kids in a 20th century style for a 21st century world.

Let me provide one example of a teacher who embraced the 21st century instead of shunning the current culture. Karl Fisch is a 20-year veteran of Arapahoe High School, located south of Denver, Colorado, just fifteen minutes from where I used to live. He teaches an algebra course to 9th and 10th graders (14 and 15 year-olds). However, instead of lecturing about polynomials and exponents during class time—then giving his students 30 problems to work on at home—Fisch has flipped the sequence. He's recorded his lectures on video and uploaded them to YouTube for his students to watch at home. Then, in class, he works with students as they solve problems and experiment with concepts.

Lectures at night, "homework" during the day. Call it the Fisch Flip. "When you do a standard lecture in class, and then the students go home to do the problems, some of them are lost. They spend a whole lot of time being frustrated and even worse, doing it wrong.

The idea behind the videos was to flip it. The students can watch it outside of class, pause it, replay it, view it several times, even mute me if they want," says Fisch, who emphasizes that he didn't come up with the idea, nor is he the only teacher in the country giving it a try. "That allows us to work on what we used to do as homework when I'm there to help students and they're there to help each other," he explains.

When he puts it like that, you want to slap your forehead at the idea's simple logic. You wonder why more schools aren't doing it this way. It melts traditional thinking and leads to solutions that are easy to envision and to implement.

Our Dilemma: Right-Brained Students Attend Left-Brained Schools

Let's discuss how education primarily takes place and why it fails to be effective.

Students Today	Schools Today
1. Right-brained thinkers	1. Left-brained delivery
2. Learn by uploading; expressing themselves	2. Teach by downloading lectures
3. Experiential in nature	3. Passive in nature
4. Music and art enables them to retain information	4. Music and art classes have been cut
5. Desire to learn what is relevant to life	5. Teach for the next test
6. Creativity drives them	6. Curriculum drives them

Perhaps this is why George Santayana said, "A child educated only in school is an uneducated child." Those of us who teach and train students must turn a corner—and transform the way we deliver our content. Lesson plans cannot be taught the way we did in 1989. Or even 1999. The culture has changed. Obviously, the left-brain is important, especially in certain professions. But the best leaders—regardless of their industry—learn to combine the strength of both the left and right brain. Consider Albert Einstein again. His expertise was math and science. We'd all agree those are left-brain industries. However, no one had a greater appreciation for imagination and creativity other than Albert Einstein. These are right-brain activities. Let me suggest the following:

- Teaching must not merely supply information for students, but inspiration for students.

- Teaching must do more than measure a kid's memory; it must motivate a kid's imagination.

- Teachers must include not just the facts of history, but the feelings that history produced.

- Teachers should not be reduced to increasing intelligence, but increasing innovation.

- Teaching cannot be only about what to think, but how to think.

Are You Relevant?

Pause and evaluate your teaching methods. Are you primarily a left-brain or a right-brain teacher? Are you balanced in your approach? Are you preparing students in a relevant way for the real world they will enter soon? Do you look for creative ways to deliver content?

I've been working to incorporate the "right-brain" in my teaching for several years now. When I began creating the *Habitudes®* curriculum in 2004, my goal was to communicate timeless principles in a relevant, right-brain fashion. *Habitudes®* are images that form leadership habits and attitudes. They teach life and leadership principles with images, questions, stories, and exercises. The books are short. They do not feel like textbooks. They allow teachers, coaches, parents, employers, and youth workers to put their training on ICE:

I – Images, which lead to...
C – Conversations, which lead to...
E – Experiences

This is how students learn. The age-old saying, "A picture is worth a thousand words" is based on right-brain expression. When students talk about the *Habitudes®* images, they get to "upload" their own thoughts instead of enduring the usual "download" teaching style they often experience in school or church. Finally, the conversation leads to an experience they share together. And experience changes us. To see an example of this right-brain set of books and DVDs—go to: www.Habitudes.org.

Guiding Principles for Leader Development

This is why we believe schools and organizations must embrace a 21st century understanding of students and apply a philosophy that is both relevant and lasting.

In fact, I believe an organization's philosophy of leader development can be understood by viewing the methods it employs. Just watch what an organization does from day-to-day. Then, weigh their methods against the statements provided below. They are statements describing what we believe about leader development, and why we've embrace the methods we embrace at Growing Leaders, Inc.

What We Believe About Leader Development

1. It is an inside job before it is an outside job.

A potential leader has much to learn about skills, techniques, and tactics. However, we believe the development journey must begin with working on the heart and mind of a leader. They must think like a leader before they act like one. Perspective before practice. It's a change from the inside out, not vice versa. We build leaders from the inside out so they can turn their world upside down.

2. It is a process more than an event.

It is tempting to plan an annual leadership training event, and believe it will motivate and train leaders for the year. Evidence shows this is just not true. Leader development can be ignited at a conference, but real change takes place in a community in the weeks that follow. It's an unglamorous process where reflection and practice occur and habits and attitudes are formed.

3. It is a right-brain function before it is a left-brain function.

Today's young leader has grown up in a right-brain world, but they are often forced to learn in a left-brain school. The idea of being a leader must first capture their imagination before it can engage their intellect. The use of images, conversations, and experiences casts vision into the hearts of young leaders that gives incentive to them for learning effective leadership.

4. It is more about a disposition than a position.

Too many assume leading is about holding a position on a team. If people wait to learn leadership until they have a position, they won't be ready for what lies ahead. We believe people can influence from anywhere in an organization, and the journey begins with seeing the world through the eyes of a leader. It's a perception before it's a position. Only then are they ready for a position.

5. It is learned through both uploading and downloading.

Emerging leaders have grown up in a world where they've been invited to "upload" their thoughts; to participate, to weigh in, vote, and express themselves. This is how they learn. This isn't achieved by listening to a lecture downloaded from an instructor, but through interaction and conversation. We believe there is no life change without life exchange. They learn best in circles, not rows.

6. It is about an experience, not just an explanation.

Dr. Leonard Sweet, noted educator and futurist, calls today's generation E.P.I.C. They are experiential, participatory, image-rich, and connected. Most are kinesthetic learners. They learn best by doing something. Engaging in activity has always made learning more memorable than listening in a classroom. Schools around the world that have excelled utilize experiential learning models.

7. It is about relationships before it is about results.

While effective leadership involves both relationships and results, we believe team members and target customers must see the priority of relationships first. People will go along with a leader if they get along with a leader. In fact, a mentor of young leaders must build bridges of relationship that can bear the weight of truth. This enables production. Relationships sustain long-term results.

For Discussion

1. Are you a more left-brain person or a right-brain person?
2. Do you ever observe a difference between the way you teach and the way students learn? Where is the gap?
3. What can you do to engage the student with an upload, right-brain style?
4. How are you utilizing right-brain creativity as you equip your leaders?

What Does the Leader Development Process Look Like?

As a kid, before I became a type one diabetic, I loved cotton candy. It was the snack of choice when our family visited a theme park or local carnival. For me, there was nothing like a huge swirl of blue or pink cotton candy on a hot summer day walking between Tomorrowland and the Matterhorn at Disneyland. One afternoon, my sister couldn't finish her cotton candy. Naturally, I offered to finish it for her. I had just downed mine and had no idea how a second helping would impact my stomach-I soon found out. I got sicker than a dog. It was an awful way to spend an afternoon.

I have since come to understand the true value of cotton candy. It is a tasty treat in small doses. It's delicious, but it was never intended to be a nutritious meal. It's sugar for Pete's sake. It's a dessert. You don't continue eating it until you're full. In fact, it disintegrates when it hits your tongue or fingers. It just doesn't last long and cannot fill you up.

I could say the same things about leadership training events hosted by schools, organizations, and companies across the United States. Executives make the mistake I did with cotton candy. We overdose on events that can never actually nourish us. They motivate, but they can't mature someone in their leadership skills. And the event evaporates quickly. I bet that annual conference you just attended is nothing but a great memory in the minds of your team members. No lasting change took place. The only thing that remains is a nice notebook that now collects dust on the shelf. Events are great but they fade. Like cotton candy, we all love them—but they're sugar. They energize us, but events don't last.

Events and Process

It's not a new thought. People enjoy events because they stimulate and motivate—but we all know we need a growth process following the event if we hope to make it last. In other words, after attending a training event, most people require an on-going journey; a community of relationships where the discussion expands. In the process, people continue to talk about and apply the principles that were introduced at the event. This is how good habits begin. This is how life-change occurs. Every one of us needs a process that follows the event to seal what was learned. Look at the value of both:

The Event	The Process
1. Encourages decisions	1. Encourages development
2. Motivates people	2. Matures people
3. Is a calendar issue	3. Is a consistency issue
4. Challenges people	4. Changes people
5. Becomes a catalyst	5. Becomes a culture
6. Usually is about a big group	6. Usually is about a small group
7. Occurs at one point in time	7. Occurs over a period of time

There is nothing wrong with events. I believe, however, that students and adults require both an event as well as a follow-through process in order to grow and mature in their leadership skills. They often need a catalyst (at an event) to spark a decision, then they need a week-by-week process to implement that decision into their lives. The younger an audience is, the more they need a process to be in place to foster growth. Further, the younger an audience is, the more concrete this process must be. It cannot be abstract or conceptual. The process must be specific and intentional. Sadly, for most students, this is a luxury. We whisk them off to the next concert, retreat, conference, or convention, then we're on to a new subject. This is why so few lasting changes happen after summer youth camp. It was a great event—but there was no follow-up process to reinforce and apply what they heard.

The Non-Negotiables

So just what is required to do a leader-development process? No doubt the process can take on many forms. No two may look alike. I believe, however, the essential elements are below.

1. Community Interaction

People need to interact. They learn as much through uploading as they do from receiving a download of information from a leader. They learn best in social contexts. Engagement and ownership of the issue increases as students have the opportunity to push back and think out loud with a handful of others.

2. Relevant Resources

To insure the interaction doesn't get hijacked into a black hole, resources are helpful to furnish direction and discovery. A resource is not a "god" but a guide. It could be a book, a podcast, MP3 download, article, CD, or DVD to stimulate thoughtful reflection and discussion on the topic.

3. Facilitated Exercise

This element stimulates members of the community by involving them in more than a group discussion. It invites other senses through role-playing, case studies, activities, or hypothetical situations. By engaging their imagination, these exercises awaken their creative right-brain.

4. Real-Time Modeling

A good process always includes a leader within the community who incarnates the principle being discussed. People do what people see, the conversation gains traction. A leader provides a living example, not merely speaking words. As the saying goes, actions always speak louder.

5. Action Steps

At some point in the process, a leader should challenge the community with a real-life assignment. People must have the opportunity to practice the truth they are learning. Many students today are primarily kinesthetic learners and require activity in their growth process.

6. Measured Assessment

It has been said that experience is the best teacher. I believe evaluated experience is the best teacher, because students can easily have a bad experience and draw the wrong conclusion. Students need adults to help them process successes and failures, and draw the right life application. A process should include a time of evaluation of each student's growth.

7. Time Elapse

A process cannot take place overnight, any more than a mom or dad can parent a child overnight. Learning requires time to pass, and ideas to be digested. Most plants and animals do not grow up in a day or two. Neither do leaders. They are grown in Crockpots, not microwave ovens.

I suggest that you never plan an event unless you also plan a process to follow that event. When I visit a campus and teach leadership, our team works with the host to plan that process. When students are placed in mentoring groups for a semester, they begin to apply leadership principles to their life. The event gains traction. The groups provide accountability, support, and a laboratory to practice leadership skills with one another. Someone once said, "You can usually do less than you think you can in one week, but more than you think you can in one year." I believe the same is true about events and process. Never underestimate the power of the process. It leads to healthy growth. You might say it's like eating several good meals . . . along with some cotton candy.

A Leadership Development Process to Grow Leaders

The natural question is, "What does it look like to grow student leaders?" It means we must be intentional about both events and processes. When training student leaders, we must host "events" on our campus that also include a mentoring process. We suggest the following process in order to grow young leaders. When an organization implements this leadership development cycle, they nurture a culture of leadership. Growing Leaders can partner with you to provide tools for each step in this cycle:

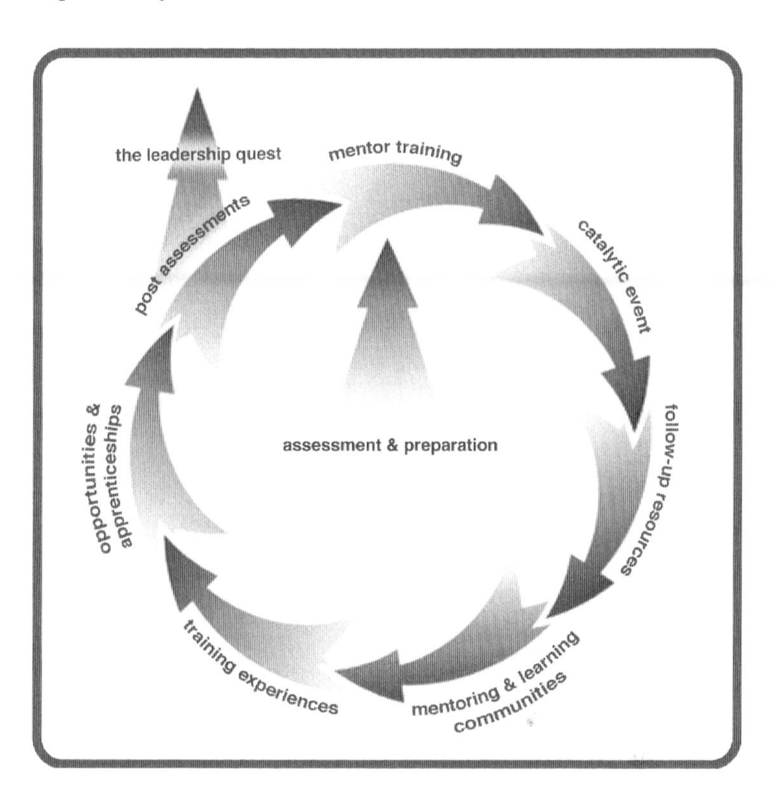

Step One: Assessment

We offer an online assessment and consultation to the needs and climate of your present situation. From this meeting, a customized plan can be created for your campus needs. Once you do this, you will have a pre-test assessment of your students at the beginning of the journey.

a. Consensus

Meet with a task force to gain consensus. Meet with staff/faculty to listen, agree on steps, and to seed the culture with leadership principles. From this meeting, plans will be communicated regarding how to nurture a leadership culture.

b. Multiplication

A key team is selected for the purpose of defining leadership, setting goals, and determining criteria for the selection of student leaders for mentoring groups.

Step Two: Mentor Training

Meet weekly with the key team to prepare them to be effective mentors. This training will equip them to lead a mentoring community after a catalytic event. The mentoring community is made up of interested students. (*Our Lifelines Training Kit* can guide you in the preparation). Key staff (campus leaders, resident directors) can go through *Habitudes #4: The Art of Changing Culture* in mentoring communities for their own leadership development. These are your core leaders.

Step Three: Catalytic Event

Hold a leadership conference on-site, to challenge students with the idea of being a leader. The goal is for the conference to be a catalyst for students to begin the leadership development process. A sample conference topic could be: *Habitudes: Images That Form Leadership Habits and Attitudes.*

Step Four: Follow-Up Resources

Depending on the need, your team should determine what resource is most relevant to guide the students' discussion in these communities. Growing Leaders offers dozens of resources you can use as guides for your students who are interested in joining a mentoring community following the event.

Step Five: Mentoring Communities – For interested students

Establish mentoring groups for the purpose of developing leadership habits and attitudes. Students who join a mentoring group will study and discuss *Habitudes #1: The Art of Self-Leadership*. This represents the "process" following the event.

- Each community is given a real-life challenge to work on during the semester.
- Each community is given a coach to lead the discovery process each week.
- Each community is exposed to consultants in the area to offer expertise from time to time.

Step Six: Mentoring Communities – For current student leaders

Establish mentoring groups for present leaders, for the purpose of equipping them to do their jobs. Student leaders should discuss *Habitudes #3: The Art of Leading Others.* This step enables leaders to remain refreshed and equipped along the way as they invest into others.

Step Seven: Training Experiences

Because leadership development is a process, not just an event, we recommend you provide ongoing training experiences for the community of leaders on your campus. These could be held weekly, twice a month, or monthly and can cover specific topics, relevant to their roles. This training can involve both instruction and application of key leadership principles.

• Communication
As mentoring groups are established, create a monthly e-mail newsletter (Leadership Insights is a suggested title) to communicate regularly with your staff and student leaders, fostering a leadership mindset among the population.

• Multiplication
In the Spring, begin the cycle of reproducing leaders, as upperclassmen and staff are ready to multiply themselves in mentoring communities.

Step Eight: Opportunities And Apprenticeships

Because students require real-life experience in order to grow, be sure and offer plenty of outlets for them to practice the leadership principles they are learning. These opportunities can be in student government, resident advisors, club leaders, mentoring community leaders, etc. Learn more about our internships at: *www.GrowingLeaders.com/internship*

Step Nine: Post-Test Assessments

Once the cycle is complete at the end of the year (or longer, depending on the school plan), a post-test is provided to assess any growth or change that has taken place among the mentors and students.

Obviously, this "cycle" is just one example of a leadership development process. While there are many variables, I suggest your administration work to include each step outlined above, to prevent a false start to the process.

In short, we must provide more than "cotton candy" to our students to stimulate their leadership growth. And we must be diligent to do the not-so-glitzy process that truly nourishes our students enabling them, to grow them into the future leaders of our world.

Laying Out a Plan for Your Campus

I'd like to help you get very practical at this point. In view of these suggested steps, our team at Growing Leaders, has created "Planning Profiles" for you. They'll provide a track for you to run on as you plan a leader development path for your administrators, staff, faculty, and students. You can download these "Planning Profiles" for free, by going to our website:

www.GrowingLeaders.com.

Just click on the tab: "Manifesto" and you'll be guided to a page with the forms and other helpful content on developing leaders.

For Discussion

1. What is your leader development process? What does it include?
2. Are you weak in any of the steps above? If so, which ones?
3. What additional step could you add this year?

The Marks of Maturity

You may have noticed a paradox that exists among students today. Although there are exceptions to the rule, this generation of kids is advanced intellectually, but behind emotionally. We have confirmed this reality from California to New York. It will likely impact where you begin your leader development plans for your students.

From an intellectual perspective, students today have been exposed to so much more than I was growing up—and far sooner, too. They've consumed information on everything from cyberspace to sexual techniques before they graduate from middle school. Everything is coming at them sooner. Sociology professor Tony Campolo said,

"I am convinced we don't live in a generation of bad kids. We live in a generation of kids who know too much too soon."

On the other hand, students have been stunted in their emotional maturity. They seem to require more time to actually "grow up" and prepare for the responsibility that comes with adulthood. This is a result of many factors, not the least of which is well-intentioned parents who hover over their kids, not allowing them to experience the pain of maturation. It's like the little boy who tries to help the new butterfly break out of the cocoon. He realizes later that he has done a disservice to that butterfly. Because of his "help," the butterfly is not strong enough to fly once it is free.

There is another reason, however, that teens struggle with maturation. Scientists are gaining new insights into remarkable changes in teenagers' brains that may explain why the teen years are so hard on young people and their parents. From ages 11-14, kids lose some of the connections between cells in the part of their brain that enables them to think clearly and make good decisions.

Pruning the Brain

What happens is that the brain is pruning itself—going through changes that will allow a young person to move into adult life effectively. "Ineffective or weak brain connections are pruned in much the same way a gardener would prune a tree or bush, giving the plant a desired shape," says Alison Gopnik, Professor of Child Development at U.C. Berkley. Adolescents who are experiencing these brain changes can react emotionally, according to Ian Campbell, a neurologist at the U.C. Davis Sleep Research Laboratory. Mood swings, uncooperative and irresponsible attitudes can all be the result of these changes occurring. Sometimes, students can't explain why they feel the way they do. Their brain is changing from a child brain to an adult brain. Regions that specialize in language, for example, grow rapidly until about age 13 and then stop. The frontal lobes of the brain which are responsible for high level reasoning and decision making aren't fully mature until the early 20s, according to Deborah Yurgelun-Todd, a neuroscientist at Harvard's Brain Imaging Center. There's a portion of time when the child part of the brain has been pruned, but the adult portion is not fully formed. They are "in-between." They are informed but not prepared.

The bottom line? Students today are consuming information they aren't completely ready to handle. The adult part of their brain is still forming and isn't ready to apply all that our society throws at it. Their mind takes it in and files it, but their will and emotions are not prepared to act on it in a healthy way. They can become paralyzed by all the content they consume. They want so much to be able to experience the world they've seen on websites and television, but don't realize they are unprepared for that experience emotionally. They are truly in between a child and an adult. (This is the genius behind movie ratings and viewer discretion advisories on TV). I believe a healthy, mature student is one who has developed intellectually, volitionally, emotionally, and spiritually. I also believe there are marks we can look for, as we coach them into maturity.

Obviously, as we develop student leaders, one of the first characteristics we want them to model is maturity. They should be role-models for the student body. Before they ever cultivate speaking skills, or organizational skills—these young leaders should be pictures of maturity, ideally.

Signs to Look For

So what are the marks of maturity? We all love it when we see young people who carry themselves well and show signs of being mature. They interact with adults in an adult manner. Those kinds of students are downright refreshing. Let me give you a list of what I consider to be the marks of maturity. At Growing Leaders we seek to build these marks in young people, ages 16-24, as we partner with schools. This certainly isn't an exhaustive list, but it is a list of characteristics I notice in young people who are unusually mature, intellectually, emotionally, and spiritually. If you are a parent—this is a good list of qualities to begin developing in your child. If you are a coach, or a teacher, or a dean, these are the signs we wish every student possessed when they graduate. For that matter, these are signs I wish all adults modeled for the generation coming behind them.

1. THEY ARE ABLE TO KEEP LONG-TERM COMMITMENTS.

One key signal of maturity is the ability to delay gratification. Part of this means a student is able to keep commitments even when they are no longer new or novel. They commit to continue doing what is right even when they don't feel like it.

2. THEY ARE UNSHAKEN BY FLATTERY OR CRITICISM.

As people mature, they sooner or later understand that nothing is as good as it seems and nothing is as bad as it seems. Mature people can receive compliments or criticism without letting it ruin them or sway them into a distorted view of themselves. They are secure in their identity.

3. THEY POSSESS A SPIRIT OF HUMILITY.

Humility parallels maturity. Humility isn't thinking less of yourself. It is thinking of yourself less. Mature people aren't consumed with drawing attention to themselves. They see how others have contributed to their success and can even sincerely give honor to their Creator who gave them the talent.

4. Their decisions are based on character not feelings.

Mature people—students or adults—live by values. They have principles that guide their decisions. They are able to progress beyond merely reacting to life's options, and they're proactive as they live their lives. Their character is master over their emotions.

5. They express gratitude consistently.

I have found the more I mature, the more grateful I am, for both big and little things. Immature children presume they deserve everything good that happens to them. Mature people see the big picture and realize how good they have it, compared to most of the world's population.

6. They prioritize others before themselves.

A wise man once said, "A mature person is one whose agenda revolves around others, not self." Certainly this can go to an extreme and be unhealthy, but I believe a pathway out of childishness is getting past your own desires and beginning to live to meet the needs of others less fortunate.

7. They seek wisdom before acting.

Finally, a mature person is teachable. They don't presume they have all the answers. The wiser they get, the more they realize they need more wisdom. They're not ashamed of seeking counsel from adults, whether they be parents, teachers, coaches, or pastors. Only the wise seek wisdom.

For Discussion

1. Based on this list, are you mature?
2. How about your students?
3. What qualities do you try to nurture in the students you teach?

Growing Convergent Leaders

As you consider how to grow leaders on your campus, it's important to further clarify what you're shooting for. Examine your current results. What are the common denominators your leaders enjoy? What is the product of your efforts? Is leading about gaining power? Is it about the command and control of people? Or, is it healthy, life-giving leadership; something more rare and attractive to our world today?

Why is it we often see students running from the idea of being a "leader?" What is it that comes to their mind that often causes a hesitation, or worse, a retreat? Why do so many talented and smart students fail to reach their leadership potential?

The answer may be tucked away somewhere inside the principle of the "convergent leader." I believe talent, IQ, and low expectations aren't the only factors in why people fail to realize their potential. Often, young people are one dimensional in their thinking. They don't see the whole picture. There are at least four elements that determine career outcomes for emerging leaders. When these elements converge together, young people are able to reach their highest level of potential.

The best leaders are convergent leaders. They know a person's success is contingent upon four ingredients converging in their lives. They flourish because they capitalize on these factors:

- Strength

Their inward abilities, made up of their talent, knowledge, gifts, and skills.

- Situation

The context and group chemistry in which they use their gifts and style.

- Style

Their outward approach or manner in which they relate to and lead teams.

- Subject

The issue or cause for which they have a high level of passion.

Let me illustrate. Sir Winston Churchill served as Prime Minister of England during the dark days of World War Two. Do you know how he got there? It was through a series of lesser roles and missteps during the 1920s and 30s. Churchill had been involved in politics early on, and had done an average job. Few saw him as a future Prime Minister. He was gruff and often offended his colleagues and constituents. However, as the Nazi regime rose to power in Germany, it became clear that Prime Minister Chamberlain and his appeasement policies were not working. Although Churchill was in the shadows, and his political career was fading in the minds of Brits, he was the perfect fit for the times. His strength was strategy and vision. He was a thoughtful planner, a decision-maker, and a compelling communicator—all crucial qualities at that time. His style was perfect for the need of the hour—to persuade the British citizens not to lose heart and to influence other nations (like the U.S.) to join them in fighting for the free world. The situation and timing was right for him, too. Churchill had served in the military, and he was comfortable during wartime. In fact, when the war ended, he was immediately removed by the British, knowing that his leadership would not be as effective during peacetime. He loved the subject (war) and the cause (freedom) and flourished in times of crisis.

There was full engagement because Churchill's strength, style, situation, and subject converged together.

Compare Winston Churchill and Mahatma Gandhi. These men stand in contrast to one another in their style, strength, and situation. Yet, both are considered remarkable leaders. Churchill's bold and commanding leadership succeeded in mobilizing a war-ravaged nation. It is unlikely he would have had much success emulating Gandhi's calm and quiet approach. Yet, Gandhi's style, a peaceful revolution during India's struggle for independence, was perfect for his time and situation. It is good he didn't try to emulate Churchill. Both men knew their strengths and style and used them wisely. Both were effective leaders, when in the right situation at the right time. How vital are these four factors—strength, style, situation, and subject? Consider these scenarios.

How important is discovering and capitalizing on one's strength's?

Just ask Julia Child, who wandered trying to find her "niche" until she discovered cooking later in her life. She was 47 when she finished her first cookbook; she wasn't on TV until she was 51. Ask Harlan Sanders who was in his 60s before he capitalized on his recipe for fried chicken . . . and became the Colonel. Or, ask Michael Jordan if strengths are important after he played a season of professional baseball.

How important is style to whether a leader flourishes?

Just ask my friend, Greg, who pastored a church in Michigan with great results. His budget, attendance, morale, and active membership rose. However, when he moved to South Carolina and employed the same style and programs, he flopped. He even questioned whether he should quit the ministry. His apparent failure was devastating to him. But it was an issue of style, not vocation.

How important is situation to a leader?

Just ask a pro athlete who was traded to another team. I've lost count of the number of good players who were traded and became great. Or, conversely, there are great players who get traded and never flourish again. The game stayed the same, but the chemistry on the team totally changed. Young Walt Disney was told he had no creativity or talent. This just wasn't true—but he needed an environment where he could flourish.

How important is subject to a leader's performance and passion?

Ask John Quincy Adams. His one-term presidency wasn't a success. Most say he floundered. Two years later he was challenged to run for Congress—seemingly a step down. But this is where he added his greatest value. Under Washington and Jefferson, character and statesmanship were a given. Launching a nation brought leaders together. Following Adams' presidency, however, the moral fiber was unraveling among bureaucrats. He became the conscience of Congress. He came alive during these latter years of his life and found his voice during his seventeen years in the House of Representatives.

Because I do leadership training in schools, I meet many young people who ask, "How can I become an effective leader?" It is an incomplete question. Leader of whom? Going where? Someone becomes the best leader by finding the right goal, context, and followers. So much is involved in successful leadership: trust, incentive, timing, gifts, and vision. Dr. Martin Luther King, Jr. could have remained a respected pastor in Atlanta, confined to and pampered by his congregation during the 1960s, but he found a different situation and context in which to lead. It enabled him to go from good to great. He was a right "fit" for the civil rights movement at the time.

When America was young, our population had two factions: those who feared the power of any leader because of their experience in England, and those who loved George Washington so much they wanted to make him king of the United States. However, it was the constitutional context and the democracy Washington helped to create that made him perfect for a presidency, not a monarchy. During his second term he drew much criticism for both his character and his policies—since so many feared he could become a king. Yet, because his style was adverse to absolute power—because he didn't seek it—he was perfect as a leader in his context. He set the precedent for a democracy.

Most people have read about the early days of the McDonald's restaurant franchise. The two brothers, Dick and Maurice McDonald, started a drive-in restaurant in Glendale, CA in 1937. Their gift was perfect for their goal: to create good food, served in a fast and friendly style. They were fast-food pioneers. However, the two brothers were unable to multiply what they had done in California. They tried and failed more than once. That's when Ray Kroc found them and offered to take over in 1955. Ray didn't possess gifts to make hamburgers or

French fries. He did, however, have a gift to franchise the idea. Perfect situation, strength, subject, and style.

What Occurs When Convergence Happens?

When a leader experiences one of these four factors, they can function. In fact, they may become satisfied with merely being functional, assuming there's nothing more to their career. When two or three factors are present, leaders become fruitful, and they see results. This increases their incentive. However, I believe leaders flourish, when all four factors are present—and those leaders are firing on all cylinders. When leaders experience all four:

THEIR CONFIDENCE GOES UP.

THEIR CAPACITY GOES UP.

THEIR INFLUENCE GOES UP.

THEIR PASSION GOES UP.

THEIR INTUITION GOES UP.

THEIR FULFILLMENT GOES UP.

Think about your own life and leadership. Do you model convergent leadership? Consider the young leaders in your life. Are they firing on all cylinders . . . or are they sputtering, trying to emulate someone else? What can you do to enable the people under you to experience convergence? Do you know their strengths, their primary style, their optimal situation, and do you know the subjects for which they are passionate? Discovering these will diminish the amount of training they require. They become natural leaders in that situation. High convergence equals high performance. For most people, convergence doesn't happen until later in life and for many, it never happens. May we help this next generation converge sooner and flourish early on their journey.

For Discussion

1. Which of the four ingredients in convergent leaders do you see most often on your campus/organization and among your students and staff?
2. Which of the four are often missing?
3. How could you create "leadership incubators" that nurture all four ingredients in your organization?

Creating a Leadership Culture

We cannot enjoy a complete discussion of this subject unless we cover the idea of a leadership culture. Years ago I came to see that simply creating a program for leader development isn't enough. When I train a set of leaders in a program, I may satisfy the need for leaders in my organization temporarily, but holes will need to be filled again next year. I must nurture a culture of leadership, where every student, staff, and teacher catches the virus.

When you raise the tide—all the boats go up. That's what a healthy culture does.

Consider this. The best way to foster certain behavior in a person is to raise them in a particular culture. For instance, in the country of Kenya, no mother must remind her child to go out each day, and "act like a Kenyan." Why? Because they are living in the Kenyan culture. It's all around them. They will most certainly emulate the culture they live in—speaking the language, adhering to the customs, and embracing the values of that culture.

The most effective schools, organizations, and companies that build leaders do so because they've nurtured a leadership culture. They aren't satisfied with finding a few leaders each year to fill the vacancies in their leadership positions. Their culture fosters leader development, and affects everyone. Keep in mind there are two kinds of changes leaders make with their teams:

PROGRAMMATIC

These are program changes. They are artificial and don't transform.

ORGANIC
These are authentic changes in the relationships and fiber of your environment.

Let's begin by asking the all-important question leaders must consider before making any changes.

Are You Building a Leadership Cult or Culture?

This question may sound extreme. Is this our only choice? Either a cult or a culture of leadership? Not exactly. However, based on your leadership—you will create an environment that leans toward one of these two below.

A CULT: A rudimentary group of people devoted to a person, whose organization fades when the personality that creates it departs.

A CULTURE: A community of people which share common language, values, and behaviors, which set them apart from others, and which grows of itself.

None of us plan to create a personal cult. We despise stories of cult leaders like Jim Jones, Charles Manson and David Koresh who led hundreds of people astray. However, when we cause others to depend solely on our leadership—we share some of the same qualities of a cult. While our message is nothing like Charles Manson's, our methods are far too similar.

The paradox at the heart of leadership is that the leader must add value to the organization but must not take it away when he or she leaves. An essential part of a leader's job is to become dispensable through creating a culture of leadership that extends throughout the campus or organization, and outlives the leader.

What Do All Cultures Share?

Think about the different cultures you visited in the past. All cultures share some common ingredients:

- COMMON VALUES-Cultures spread when people inside them incarnate values and live them out in everyday life.

- COMMON LANGUAGE-Part of what makes cultures unique is that they share a language that sets them apart.
- COMMON QUALITIES-Cultures possess qualities that are unique to them and identify them to outsiders.
- COMMON CUSTOMS AND BEHAVIORS-Finally, cultures tend to experience certain customs, behaviors and traditions

Cult	Culture
1. Emerges quickly with a forceful leader	1. Emerges slowly in time with a leadership team
2. Based on the personality of the leader	2. Based on the shared values and goals of people
3. Fragile and volatile due to the leader	3. Durable and robust due to the environment
4. Future lasts as long as the leader does	4. Future lasts as all transmit to next generation
5. People are controlled from the top	5. People are empowered from the top
6. Leader pushes values on others	6. Leaders model and teach competence, passion
7. Works through compliance	7. Works through commitment
8. Centralization (positional power)	8. De-centralization (personal power)
9. Can breed fear and insecurity	9. Will breed love and respect
10. Low risk, low reward	10. High risk, high reward
11. The leader leads followers	11. The leader creates leaders
12. Short-term success	12. Long-term success

Most organizations suffer from a chronic lack of quality leaders. Staff members often have little training in leadership. They hope that leaders will transfer from the outside, or that they'll learn leadership simply from the challenges of life. Unfortunately, it usually doesn't work that way. A leadership culture emerges when someone champions the cause of leadership and works a plan to create that environment. This is true of almost every movement in history.

What We Learn From History

Cultures arise out of movements, not programs. Programs usually start big and eventually fizzle. Movements usually start small and grow large over time. If you study how movements began in history, you find there is a pattern:

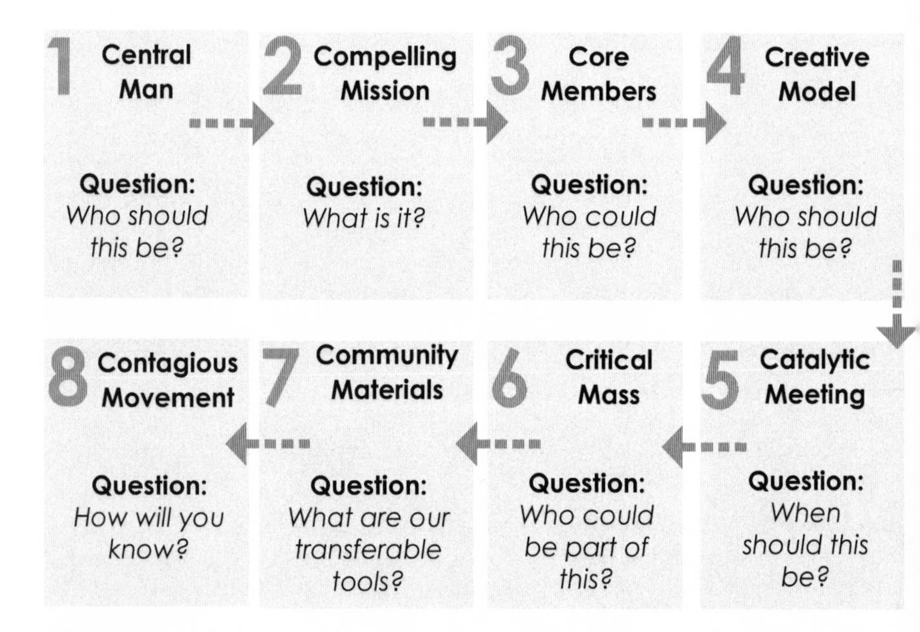

Step by Step

Real culture change often begins with a single man or woman who believes in something. They get committed to change. This individual is the pioneer who leads the way. During the 1700s, John Wesley saw the need for social and spiritual renewal in England.

Soon, this pioneer summarizes their belief into a specific mission statement that can be repeated and remembered. It is compelling and magnetic to others. Wesley's compelling message was that people must be transformed from the inside out.

Next, a handful of others join this individual and lock arms. They all see the need and want to use their gifts to bring it into reality. They become the "core." Wesley's core group include his brother Charles and future preacher, George Whitefield.

Along the way, this core group of people identify a model (or a population of people) who accomplished a similar goal in the past. This group can be emulated and provide hope. The model for Wesley's movement were the Moravians—a group in Europe who incarnated what Wesley was preaching to Great Britain.

Eventually, the people involved plan a catalytic meeting to cast vision for their big idea. This meeting is often a large event where many are exposed to the cause. John Wesley's meetings occurred in cities where he traveled in his circuit riding. He gathered a group from the city and began speaking to them about his convictions.

Following this event, a percentage of people choose to buy in. They may only be a handful of the population, but they make up a critical mass who is enough to give the idea traction. In each crowd, a small percentage stepped forward and converted. Wesley organized the into small groups, or class meetings. History tells us, however, that Wesley only got 1 ½ to 2% of the British population on board with his cause.

Ultimately, the original pioneer or member of the core puts the cause into print. They record the big idea so that the message can become viral and outlive the original core. Along the way, John Wesley began putting his core ideas into books which made their way around the class meetings.

Finally, this vision becomes reality for a population of people over time. The idea is fulfilled. What was once only a concept in the mind of a person is now contagious. In Wesley's case, he was so methodical in organizing people, he was called the Great Methodist. John Wesley was the founder of the Methodist Church, which still exists to this day.

Leadership Culture (n): An environment of shared values and behaviors that contagiously affect students to think and act like servant leaders.

Changing the Culture

Leaders who revolutionize what's going on in their organizational culture practice the following elements:

1. MODEL

They determine to model the very behavior and performance they expect the team to emulate.

2. MEASURE

They measure the behaviors they want everyone to practice, knowing what gets measured gets done.

3. MANAGE

They give careful attention and monitoring to the behaviors and values they want others to embrace.

4. MOTIVATE

They find ways to reward and encourage, and thus, motivate team members to practice the values.

For more practical steps to cultivating a leadership culture, see the end of this *Manifesto,* where I suggest a variety of resources on this subject.

Here's to hoping you will accomplish more than a program on your campus or in your organization. May you pursue a movement that outlives you.

For Discussion

1. Have you seen a movement before? Did you participate? What was it like?
2. Describe your current culture on your campus or in your organization?
3. What are your next steps to creating a leadership culture?

Connecting with the Next Generation of Leaders

As we close this *Manifesto*, we'd be amiss if we didn't cover a most important topic. In fact, without mastering this topic, none of the previous ideas will succeed.

Stop and reflect for a minute. Think about the way you lead people. Especially students. What's your style?

Over the past few years, as I travel the road and speak in schools, companies, and other organizations, I have purposefully observed thousands of leaders do their thing. I've drawn several conclusions, and some have proven to be helpful, fresh insights for me. Let me toss one of them to you here:

Your motivation for leading will determine your:

DURATION
If your motive is good, it will impact how long you last.

DONATION
If your motive is good, it will increase the value you add to the team.

DECISIONS
If your motive is good, it will enhance your wisdom and objectivity.

DIRECTION
If your motive is good, it will determine your style and approach.

In other words—why you do something will ultimately determine what you do as a leader. Let me illustrate with the following popular styles of leadership. I suggest how motivation fits into the style and decisions of each type of leader.

Commanders

You know these people. They lead with a top-down style. Their behavior is marked by one-way communication. They download only. It's one person leveraging their power over the team. They may have begun their leadership journey in a different style, but as they aged or grew impatient with people, they got short and migrated to a "just do what I want you to do" style. It's an approach that's more about telling than asking. It's about demanding and requiring. You don't have to be a psychologist to see that this leader's motives are distorted. Commanders operate from a desire for power. Their goal is to enforce their rules and authority.

Commanders want CONTROL.

Kings

Kings represent a slightly different style of leader. Their behavior is marked by a drive to maintain stability. Why? Because stability is the best way to remain king. They have a growing love for tradition; they have a vested interest in keeping things the way they've been in the past. It's as though once this leader got the position—the entire goal is to keep the position. These leaders are about managing stuff. They want order. They aren't necessarily bad people, but they are likely going to be bad leaders in our ever-changing world. Kings are compromisers. They won't take risks unless the risk is about helping to maintain and manage what already exists. The goal of the monarchy is to enrich the king; to keep him in power.

Kings want COMPLIANCE.

Celebrities

Celebrities are a third type of leadership style. Their behavior is marked by the pursuit of perks and popularity. If you watch them closely, you'll notice a keen desire for applause and affirmation. Like the styles above, they aren't necessarily bad people, but this motivation for recognition not only diminishes their ability to lead well, it clouds their ability to make good decisions. Their perspective is colored by their own needs. They want to be noticed. They're the proverbial "YouTube" video maker who posts videos to see how many people watch them. Celebrities love accumulating friends in a Facebook group. Because this is their motive, they want peace between all parties. They want folks to get along, be happy, and look to them for entertainment and fulfillment. They love the fame that comes with their position. They love the attention it affords them.

The celebrity leader wants CREDIT.

So What Can We Do?

Although each of these styles is common, they represent unhealthy leadership. Perhaps you have identified with one of them, but today's leader must emerge out of these ineffective styles, especially if we want to lead the next generation. I don't know of any young person today who is looking for a leader who is a "commander" or a "king" or a "celebrity." In those styles, students can sense that motives are wrong and that progress and purpose are diminished because of the leader.

So, what can we do to grow healthy leaders? What do we need to change? How should we target our leadership so it is relevant and healthy for a new generation who looks for good leadership? Let me suggest a fourth style that I've observed most young people today are looking for in a leader.

Connectors

If leaders will shift their motives away from themselves and their own needs, they will find their style will shift as well. I call the new kind of leaders, "Connectors." The Connector is healthy and doesn't need the team to affirm their value. It isn't about them. Instead, it is about connecting the players on the team in four ways:

- The leader connects team members to a "cause."
- The leader connects team members to other people on the team.
- The leader connects team members to their strengths.
- The leader connects relationally to each of the team members.

This is not to say Connecters fail to run point. They are definitely responsible for the outcomes. But they know it is a team effort, and their job is to maximize the potential of each team member. This means they understand they lead in an "upload" culture, not merely a "download" one, which only allows the leader to have a say. Connectors help their team members flourish. Their goal is to turn potential into performance, regardless of who gets the credit. It means the leader recognizes the value of relationships between team members, not just their relationship to their team members. It means they share the power. The columns below summarize the shift from yesterday's leadership style to today's prototype:

Yesterday's Leader	Today's Leader
1. Uses threats to move people	1. Uses passion to move people
2. Intimidating	2. Inspiring
3. It's about the company	3. It's about the cause
4. Tradition	4. Ideas
5. Steady	5. Dynamic
6. Bureaucracy	6. Innovation
7. Download	7. Upload
8. Control people	8. Connect people

Connectors create a culture where everyone wins.

This kind of leader is described in detail in *Habitudes #4: The Art of Changing Culture*. In it I talk about the leader who connects team members in order to nurture a healthy culture. If you're interested in discussing this with your team, you may want to grab a copy.

So, what's your motive for leading? Here's hoping you can move from a commander, or king or celebrity to a connector . . . for the sake of the cause and for your sake as well.

Connecting with Images, Conversations and Experiences

The reason our organization, Growing Leaders, created the *Habitudes* series is to connect with students in a language and style they understand. *Habitudes* are images that form leadership habits and attitudes.

They represent a four-book series, with thirteen engaging images in each book. These books enable you to teach timeless leadership principles with the power of an image, a conversation, and an experience.

1. Start with an image. This generation is visual and grew up with video games, television, iPods, computers, and multiple kinds of screens.

2. This leads to a conversation. Because a picture really is worth a thousand words, the natural progression is for students to discuss how that image speaks to them.

3. Finally, this leads to an experience. Experiences follow interaction, and this step is where lives begin to change—through real-life experiences and application.

Habitudes, of course, are just one example of how to connect with students. But after seeing over 300,000 students go through the books and videos—we've found they are a natural way to equip students (who have grown up in a right-brain, upload world) to build healthy leadership habits and attitudes.

Habitudes are now available in digital form, posters, podcasts, books and a three-credit leadership survey course. You can find them at: *www.GrowingLeaders.com*

Ready or Not

I am hopeful that some of these ideas have sparked new thoughts and plans for you as you invest in students on your campus. Whether you work in a school, at a non-profit organization, a company or a ministry, we believe developing the next generation of leaders is a paramount issue. Over the next fifteen years, 45% of America's workforce will be departing. Baby Boomers continue to retire each year. Even if everyone within the following demographic, Generation X, was a brilliant leader, there would not be enough of them to fill the vacancies left by the Boomers. Young adults, in Generation Y, will need to fill those spots, ready or not. I say let's get them ready.

Thank you for your investment and heart to develop this next generation. It would be a privilege to serve you and your leaders in any way possible as you continue to nurture a leadership culture in your organization or on your campus.

Tim Elmore
President
Growing Leaders

Further Resources to Help You

This Manifesto is simply a guide to spark conversation and planning. Growing Leaders has created other resources that play a specific role in the cultivation of a leadership culture. Some of them are listed below.

HABITUDES®: IMAGES THAT FORM LEADERSHIP HABITS AND ATTITUDES. (This series is available in books, videos and digital downloads).

- The Art of Self-Leadership (Volume One)
- The Art of Connecting with Others (Volume Two)
- The Art of Leading Others (Volume Three)
- The Art of Changing Culture (Volume Four)

LEADERS EVERYWHERE

This book walks a leader through how to nurture a leadership culture and build leaders at every level of the organization. Told in parable form, it tells the story of what two leaders discover as they attempt to build new leaders. (Faith-based resource)

LIFE GIVING MENTORS

This book is an encyclopedia on how to establish effective, life-giving relationships. It is a question and answer resource for organizations that wish to create a structure of developmental relationships on campus.

LIFELINES: MENTOR TRAINING DVD KIT

This DVD Training Kit provides five discs, a leader's guide, and lesson handouts for an organization to use to prepare teachers, staff, and upperclassmen to mentor younger students.

GENERATION iY—OUR LAST CHANCE TO SAVE THEIR FUTURE

This book is a manual on understanding the latest batch of kids from Generation Y, the students born since 1990, who've been raised on-line and impacted by the "I" world. It lays out a plan to lead, teach, and coach them.

NURTURING THE LEADER WITHIN YOUR CHILD

This book describes for parents and teachers how to uncover the natural style and influence of children, from ages 5 to 22. It is full of ideas and steps to take to help cultivate the best version of that child possible.

LEVERAGING YOUR INFLUENCE

This workbook is an interactive guide to lay out a plan for student leadership development on a campus or in a youth group. It furnishes a step by step plan on the stations leaders must visit on their journey to become healthy leaders.

Growing Leaders
270 Scientific Drive NW
Suite 10
Norcross, Georgia 30092
www.GrowingLeaders.com
770.495.3332